WELBECK
CHILDREN'S BOOKS

First published in Great Britain in 2024 by Welbeck Children's Books
An imprint of Hachette Children's Group
Text © 2024 Simon Mugford
Design & Illustration © 2024 Dan Green

ISBN: 978 1 80453 677 3

Writer: Simon Mugford
Designer and Illustrator: Dan Green
Designer: Arvind Shah
Design Manager: Sam James
Senior Commissioning Editor: Suhel Ahmed
Production: Melanie Robertson

FSC
www.fsc.org
MIX
Paper | Supporting
responsible forestry
FSC® C104740

Printed in Dongguan, China
10 9 8 7 6 5 4 3 2 1

Statistics and records correct as of July 2023

Welbeck Children's Books
An imprint of Hachette Children's Group
Part of Hodder & Stoughton Limited
Carmelite House, 50 Victoria Embankment
London EC4Y 0DZ

An Hachette UK Company
www.hachette.co.uk
www.hachettechildrens.co.uk

SOCCER STORIES

MESSI

SIMON MUGFORD

DAN GREEN

Look out!

Here comes little Lionel Messi. This boy from Argentina grew up to be one of the greatest footballers ever.

How did he get there?

Let's find out.

As soon as he could walk, Messi started playing soccer in the park. Everyone called him "Titch" because he was very young and small, but that didn't stop Messi.

At school, Messi played soccer during recess. None of his friends could get near him when he had the ball!

The soccer team where Messi lived was called Newell's Old Boys, and it was Messi's dream to play for them one day. When Messi was six, his dream came true.

As Messi got better and better at soccer, Newell's Old Boys would win matches by more and more goals.

Sometimes they beat teams by 15 or more goals!

Messi even entertained the crowd
with juggling at half time.

This is Messi's grandmother, Celia. She took Messi to soccer training and matches when he was young, and she was always there to cheer him on.

When Messi was 10, Celia passed away and Messi was terribly sad. From then on, Messi often pointed his fingers towards the sky when he scored a goal.

That was to remember Celia.

Messi's dad went to live in Barcelona
with him, but Messi still really missed
the rest of his family and his friends.

Gerard

Cesc

Messi felt much happier when he made friends
with these two other Barcelona players.
They are Gerard Pique and Cesc Fabregas.

He had to wear a face mask in the 2003 Catalan cup because he was still healing from an injury. He couldn't see very well in it, so he took it off. Then he scored twice in 10 minutes! People called that special match "The Game of the Mask".

A year later, when he was just 17, Messi became part of Barcelona's first team. Now he was playing in La Liga—the best soccer league in Spain.

This is Ronaldinho. He was Barcelona's superstar goal scorer at the time. He became good friends with Messi and called him his "little brother".

Ronaldinho set up Messi's very first La Liga goal. Together with another striker called Samuel Eto'o, Ronaldinho and Messi made an awesome attacking trio!

Messi also played brilliantly with Barcelona's star players Xavi Hernandez and Andres Iniesta. They played in the middle of the pitch, passing the ball to Messi so he could score goals.

Back then, the team's manager was Pep Guardiola. He taught his players to move and pass the ball quickly so they could always hold onto it in games. Spanish people called this way of playing "Tiki-taka".

TIKI-TAKA WORKED!

For 11 years, Messi's Barcelona team were La Liga champions seven times and they won lots of cups.

Then Messi joined forces with Luis Suárez and Neymar to form a new attacking super team. Everyone called them "MSN". They played together for three seasons.

In their very first season together, MSN won three of the greatest soccer titles in the world! They won La Liga, a Spanish cup tournament called Copa del Rey, and the Champions League in Europe.

Suárez

Neymar

MSN scored 364 goals between them, and helped to set up another 211 goals. They were unstoppable!

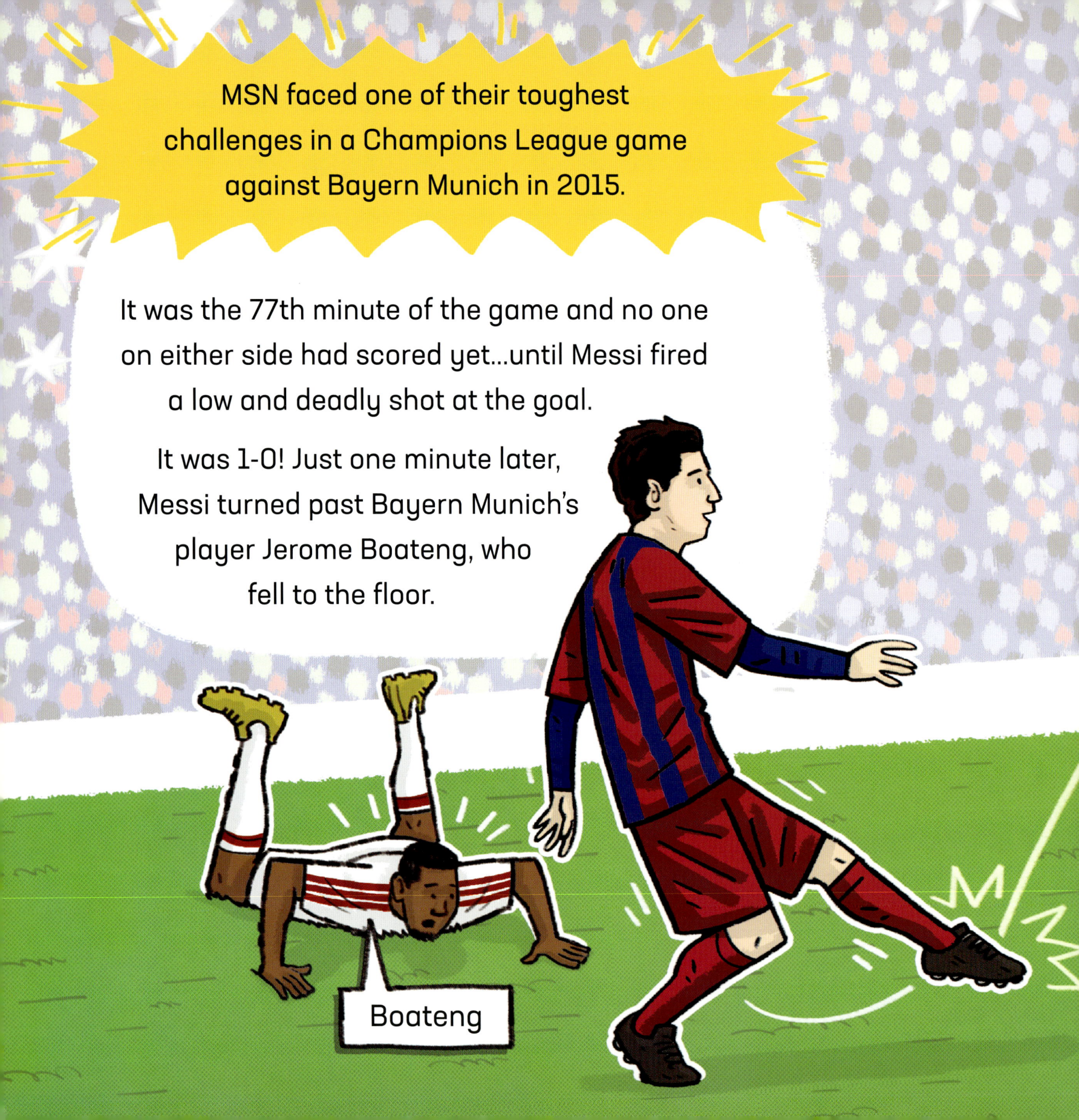

MSN faced one of their toughest challenges in a Champions League game against Bayern Munich in 2015.

It was the 77th minute of the game and no one on either side had scored yet...until Messi fired a low and deadly shot at the goal.

It was 1-0! Just one minute later, Messi turned past Bayern Munich's player Jerome Boateng, who fell to the floor.

Boateng

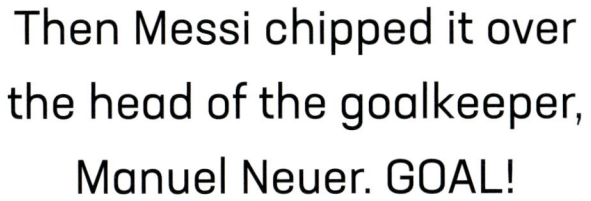

Then Messi chipped it over the head of the goalkeeper, Manuel Neuer. GOAL!

The score was 2-0. Then Neymar made it 3-0, and Bayern Munich were finished.

Neuer

Messi made history with Barcelona time and time again, and he broke tons of La Liga records.

With Messi on their side, Barcelona won the treble—La Liga, the Copa del Rey, and the Champions League—not once, but twice!

In 17 seasons, Messi scored an incredible 474 goals for Barcelona in La Liga. No one has ever scored more La Liga goals than Messi!

Messi is also a World Champion. He has played for Argentina more than any other player. He is their captain and their top goal scorer.

Messi became an Olympic gold medallist with the team in the 2008 Olympic Games.

In 2021, Messi's Argentina team beat Brazil in the Copa América final.

Then, just a year later, Argentina finally won the big one: the World Cup! Messi scored twice in the final against France.

Messi's biggest rival is Cristiano Ronaldo.

When Ronaldo played for the Spanish team Real Madrid, Messi played against him many times in La Liga.

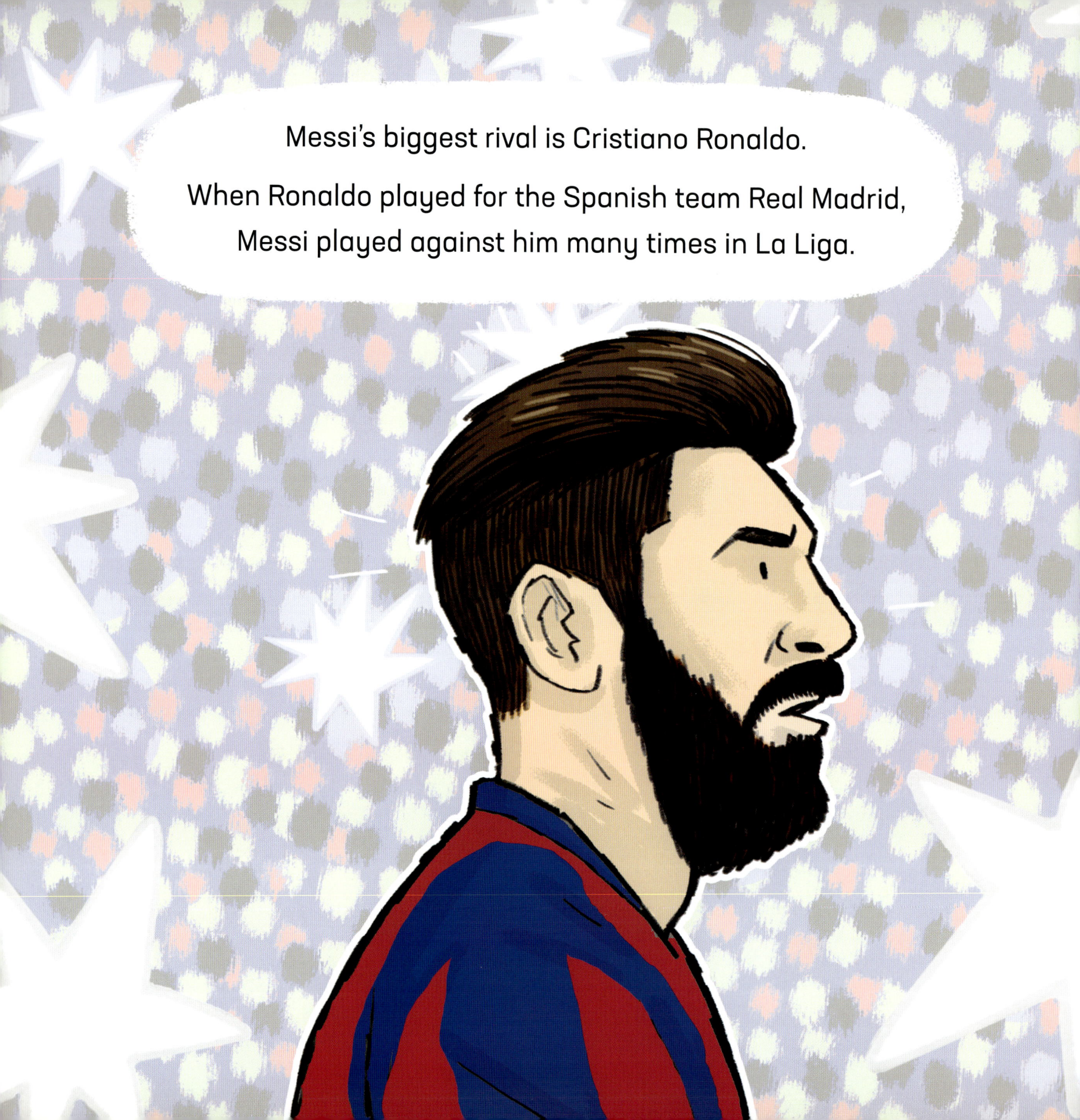

They raced to beat each other's goal scoring records, and to win the Ballon d'Or (The Golden Ball) - a prize awarded to the best soccer player in the world each year.

The argument about who's the best will go on forever! Who do you think is the best?

Messi disappointed all Barcelona fans in 2021 when he left the club! He joined the French team Paris St Germain.

Then, at the end of that year, he broke another incredible record: he won the Ballon d'Or for a seventh time.

Messi moved again in 2023. This time he moved to the US to play for Inter Miami, where he had spectacular success!

Who knows what will happen next in Messi's career?

One thing is for sure: Messi will go down in history as one of the greatest ever soccer players.